THE **DANIEL**PLAN FIVE ESSENTIALS SERIES

# FRIENDS

# THE DANIEL PLAN | FIVE ESSENTIALS SERIES

# FRIENDS

*Essential Five*

## ENCOURAGING EACH OTHER

STUDY GUIDE                                    FOUR SESSIONS

*featuring*

# DR. JOHN TOWNSEND
# & DEE EASTMAN
*with* KAREN LEE-THORP

**ZONDERVAN®**

ZONDERVAN

*Friends Study Guide*
Copyright © 2015 by The Daniel Plan

This title is also available as a Zondervan ebook. Visit www.zondervan.com/ebooks.

Requests for information should be addressed to:
Zondervan, 3900 *Sparks Dr. SE, Grand Rapids, Michigan 49546*

ISBN 978-0-310-82348-3

*Cover photography: iStockphoto*
*Interior photography: Robert Ortiz, Kent Cameron, Don Haynes, Robert Hawkins, Shelly Antol, Matt Armendariz,*
*    the PICS Ministry at Saddleback Church, iStockphoto*
*Interior design: Kait Lamphere*

First Printing May 2015 / Printed in the United States of America

# Contents

# Welcome Letter

I am so glad you have joined us for this Daniel Plan study. I am excited for your journey, as I have seen firsthand that change is within reach as you embrace the Daniel Plan lifestyle. This groundbreaking program will equip you with practical tools to bring health into every area of your life. It has been transformative for thousands of people around the world and can be for you as well.

I speak from experience. I've not only witnessed endless stories of life change but have personally benefited from these Daniel Plan Essentials for many years now. Working full-time with five grown children, including identical triplet girls, I understand what it is like to juggle many priorities and have my health impacted. The key elements of The Daniel Plan have been completely restorative in my life as I have integrated them one step at a time.

As you go through this four-week study, the perfect complement to maximize your success is reading *The Daniel Plan: 40 Days to a Healthier Life*. The book includes a 40-day food and fitness guide, complete with a meal plan, recipes, shopping lists, and exercises that will energize your efforts. It will complement any of The Daniel Plan studies you dive into. There are also numerous articles and free resources on our website (www.danielplan.com), along with a weekly newsletter filled with tools and inspiration to keep you flourishing.

Congratulations on taking the next step to gaining vitality in your life. My prayer is that you will be inspired and fully equipped to continue your journey, and that you will experience a whole new level of wellness in the process. I pray that you will feel God's presence and will be reenergized to follow all he has planned for you.

For His Glory,

*Dee Eastman*

Dee Eastman
Founding Director, The Daniel Plan

# How to Use This Guide

There are five video studies in The Daniel Plan series, one for each of the five Essentials (Faith, Food, Fitness, Focus, and Friends). Each study is four sessions long. The studies may be done in any order. If your group is new, consider starting with the six-week *The Daniel Plan Study Guide* and companion DVD, which offers an overview of all five Essentials.

## GROUP SIZE

Each Daniel Plan video study is designed to be experienced in a group setting such as a Bible study, Sunday school class, or any small group gathering. To ensure that everyone has enough time to participate in discussions, it is recommended that large groups break into smaller groups of four to six people each.

## MATERIALS NEEDED

Each participant should have his or her own study guide, which includes notes for video segments, directions for activities, discussion questions, and ideas for personal application between sessions. This curriculum is best used in conjunction with *The Daniel Plan: 40 Days to a Healthier Life*, which includes a complete 40-day food and fitness guide that complements this study.

## TIMING

Each session is designed to be completed in 60 to 90 minutes, depending on your setting and the size of your group. Each video is approximately 20 minutes long.

## OUTLINE OF EACH SESSION

Each group session will include the following:

» *Coming Together.* The foundation for spiritual growth is an intimate connection with God and his family. A few people who really know you and earn your trust provide a place to experience the life Jesus invites you to live. This opening portion of your meeting is an opportunity to transition from your busy life into your group time.

In Session 1 you'll find some icebreaker questions on the session topic, along with guidelines that state the values your group will live by so that everyone feels comfortable sharing. In Sessions 2–4 you'll have a chance to check in with other group members to report praise and progress toward your goals of healthy living. You'll also be able to share how you chose to put the previous session's insights into practice—and what the results were. There's no pressure for everyone to answer. This is time to get to know each other better and cheer each other on.

» *Learning Together.* This is the time when you will view the video teaching segment. This study guide provides notes on the key points of the video teaching along with space for you to write additional thoughts and questions.

» *Growing Together.* Here is where you will discuss the teaching you watched. The focus will be on how the teaching intersects with your real life.

» *What I Want to Remember.* You'll have a couple of minutes after your discussion to write down one or two key insights from the teaching and discussion that you want to remember.

» *Better Together.* The Daniel Plan is all about transforming the way you actually live. So before you close your meeting in prayer, you'll take some time to think about how you might apply what you've discussed. Under "Next Steps" you'll find a list of things you can do to put the session's insights into practice. Then the "Food Tip of the Week" offers a bonus video with a great recipe or food idea. It is on your DVD if you want to view it together with your group. It is also available online for you to view on your own during the week. Likewise, the "Fitness Move of the Week" is a bonus video with a simple exercise you can add to your fitness practices. It, too, is on your DVD and online.

Encourage each other to be specific about one or two things you plan to do each week as next steps. Consider asking someone in the group to be your buddy to hold each other accountable. Create an atmosphere of fun and positive reinforcement.

» *Praying Together.* The group session will close with time for a response to God in prayer, thanking him for what he's doing for you and asking for his help to live out what you have learned. Ideas for group prayer, as well as a written closing prayer, are provided. Feel free to use them or not. Consider having different group members lead the prayer time.

# The Power to Transform

> "Be devoted to one
> another in love. Honor one
> another above yourselves."
> Romans 12:10

Have you ever started a diet or exercise plan but then ran out of willpower after a few months? This story is all too common. The truth is, we aren't designed to change by willpower alone. God created us to live in relationship with others, and his power to transform often comes to us through other people. That's why friends are the secret superfood of The Daniel Plan. We need people in our lives who will offer us essential nutrients like support and feedback.

In this study on Friends, we'll learn about the kinds of relationships that support lasting change. We'll begin in this session by looking at the first fundamental ingredient in a healthy relationship: the freedom to be vulnerable.

# COMING
# TOGETHER

If this is your first time meeting together as a group, take a moment to introduce yourself.

Also, pass around a sheet of paper on which each person can write his or her name, address, phone number, and email address. Ask for a volunteer to type up the list and email it to everyone else this week.

Finally, you'll need some simple group guidelines that outline values and expectations. See the sample in the Appendix and make sure that everyone agrees with and understands those expectations.

When you're finished with these introductory activities, give everyone a chance to respond to this icebreaker question:

> » Share about a time when a friend helped you accomplish a task or reach a goal. What happened? What did he or she do to help? How did the experience affect your friendship?

# LEARNING
# TOGETHER

## AN INTERVIEW WITH Dr. John Townsend

Play the video segment for Session 1. As you watch, use the outline provided to follow along or to take additional notes on anything that stands out to you.

» Friends are essential because:

- Real friends go deep with each other by offering grace and truth.

- People with real friends live longer.

- God created us as relational beings.

» The grace of God often comes to us through the body of Christ—his people.

» Real friends give us nutrients like eye contact, listening, support, validation, comfort, enthusiasm, identification with pain, wisdom, and feedback.

» We need to be intentional in choosing our friends. We need to identify those people who have the character qualities that will make us better people. We need people who will give to us and who will let us give to them.

» We need to be vulnerable to friends, not just to God and our spouse. We need to open up about our weakness (brokenness) and need (for care and support).

» Shame makes us fear being vulnerable, but vulnerability should become our new normal.

» To find out if someone deserves to be trusted as a real friend, we can say, "Sometimes I struggle with _____." They will either:

  • Change the subject.

  • Give advice.

  • Move toward us by giving eye contact and saying, "Tell me more" and "Me too."

» Community helps us change by creating new norms. Every community creates norms. If the people we surround ourselves with don't want to be real or change, we'll norm there. If they do want to be real and change, we'll norm there.

# GROWING
# TOGHER

Discuss what you learned from the video. Don't feel obliged to answer every question. Select those that most resonate with your group.

A *norm* is a way of doing something that is common or expected. It's what feels normal. How have the people in your life—both in the past and in the present—created the norms of the way you …

» eat?

» exercise?

» conduct your spiritual life?

Norms grow when we follow someone's example. What norms would you like your friends to have with regard to …

» eating?

» exercise?

» relating to God?

» relating to others?

When someone shares a weakness or a need, why is it more helpful to say, "Tell me more" than to give advice? How are these two responses different?

 Why, according to Scriptures such as John 13:34 and Galatians 6:2, do we need to open up to our friends about our needs and weaknesses?

> *"Love one another. As I have loved you,*
> *so you must love one another."*
>
> John 13:34

> *"Carry each other's burdens, and in this*
> *way you will fulfill the law of Christ."*
>
> Galatians 6:2

 How can we support a friend who chooses to be vulnerable to us? How might we better live out the words of the following New Testament passage?

> *"Therefore encourage one another and build each*
> *other up, just as in fact you are doing."*
>
> 1 Thessalonians 5:11

**Note:** If your group has been together for several weeks and you feel you are ready to go deeper with each other, you can take the rest of your group discussion time on question 6. Everyone should feel free to pass if they don't want to share anything. The group leader will need to decide how much airtime is available for each person. Remember that "Tell us more" is a more helpful response than giving advice. Remember also the group guidelines in the Appendix: everything shared in the group is confidential, and everyone is committed to making your group a safe place to speak openly.

If you are just getting to know each other, people may not feel comfortable sharing very much yet. If that's the case, move on to question 7.

 What is one of your areas of weakness or need? Or what is one area you'd like support in?

 Give each person a chance to complete one or more of the following sentences. As each person responds, use the two-page chart that follows to write down how you can be a good friend to that person.

» *I feel more comfortable opening up to people when …*

» *I tend to withdraw or feel anxious when …*

» *The main thing I'm hoping to get out of this discussion of Friends is …*

» *You can help me lead a healthier life by …*

| Name | I Can Be a Friend to This Person by ... |
|------|------------------------------------------|
|      |                                          |
|      |                                          |
|      |                                          |
|      |                                          |
|      |                                          |
|      |                                          |
|      |                                          |

| Name | I Can Be a Friend to This Person by ... |
|------|------------------------------------------|
|      |                                          |
|      |                                          |
|      |                                          |
|      |                                          |
|      |                                          |
|      |                                          |
|      |                                          |

# What I Want
## *to Remember*

Complete this activity on your own.

» Briefly review the video outline and any notes you took. Review also any notes from the discussion.

» In the space below, write down the most significant thing you gained from this session—from the video or the discussion. You can share it with the group if you wish.

# BETTER
# TOGETHER

Now that you've talked about some great ideas, let's get practical—and put what you're learning into action. The Daniel Plan centers around five essential areas of health. In this study you're exploring Friends, so you can begin by identifying one or two steps you can take to deepen your relationships. Then check out the Food Tip of the Week and the Fitness Move of the Week for some fresh ideas to enrich your journey toward health in those areas. There are also many tips and tools on the danielplan.com website so you can keep growing in all of the Essentials while doing this study. Use or adapt whatever is helpful to you!

# FRIENDS
## *Next Steps*

*"And let us consider how we may spur one another on toward love and good deeds."*

Hebrews 10:24

Here are a few suggested activities to help you move forward into deeper friendships. Check one or two boxes next to the options you'd like to try — choose what works for you.

☐ Plan a meal with your group, as described in the Food Tip of the Week. It could be a soup and salad bar, a taco night, a pizza night, or a potluck. *The Daniel Plan Cookbook* has recipes for healthy pizza crust, as well as ideas for healthy toppings. It also has recipes for fish tacos, chicken tacos, veggie tacos, and fajitas. *The Daniel Plan* book has recipes for salad dressing and black bean soup. Ask for a volunteer to plan and tell each person what to bring to the meal.

☐ Find a buddy who will partner with you in getting healthy. This could be a friend to exercise with, a friend to shop with, or someone to check in with for encouragement. It might be someone in your small group. It might be a coworker — you could meet for lunch once a week to share healthy food, use your lunch hour to walk, or meet at the gym before or after work. It might be a neighbor, the parent of one of your children's classmates, or someone you know from your child's sports league.

☐ Ask a friend to go for a hike, a bike ride, a workout, or a walk.

☐ Find a friend you can trust to open up to about an area of weakness or need. Maybe you don't have any big problems in your life right now, but you could use someone who wants to know the real you. Maybe you have a need for support, validation, comfort, enthusiasm, identification with pain, wisdom, or feedback. Who do you know who might have the character qualities of a trustworthy friend? Remember, you don't have to share everything with them right away. All you have to do is initiate a time to take a walk or share a meal and then at some point mention, "Sometimes I struggle with _____" or "When I think about getting healthier in my life, what I really need is _____." Then see what they do with that information.

☐ Have a conversation with your spouse, family members, or others you share meals with about eating healthier food. What are your hopes? Their hopes? Your concerns? Their concerns? If you've already been trying this for a while, what is working? What would you like to change? How does your spouse feel about it? Remember that eye contact, listening, and saying, "Tell me more" are vital parts of being a good friend to your spouse. Try to listen with an open heart more than you talk. When it's your turn to share, aim for vulnerability rather than control by saying things like, "I long for _____," "I need _____," and "I am struggling with _____."

☐ Send a text of thanks or appreciation to someone. It could be someone who is encouraging you to get healthier, or it could be someone who has supported you in some other way. Maybe it's someone in your small group.

☐ Do you find it hard to be vulnerable with others? Read "If It's Hard for You to Be Vulnerable" in the Appendix. Spend some time reflecting on whether shame is a barrier for you in relationships. If it is, you may be embarrassed to talk with someone about it, but you need to break the habit of isolation. Identify someone in your group or your church who is likely to be a safe person to open up to. Try inviting them to join you for a meal, and when you get together, show an interest in the other person's life, but also decide to be honest about your response to this session's teaching on vulnerability. See if they show an interest in hearing more, and if they do, you can follow up.

# Food Tip
## *of the Week*

The "secret sauce" of The Daniel Plan is not a recipe in the cookbook but the joy of sharing a meal—and our journey—with friends. Eating together lifts our spirits and gives us a sense of well-being. This week's tip will help you plan a healthy meal for a group. Just click the Food Tip of the Week on your video screen (3 minutes), scan the QR code, or go to danielplan.com/foodtip.

# Fitness Move
## *of the Week*

Does your gluteus maximus need a lift? Of course it does! Learn how by clicking the Fitness Move of the Week on your video screen (1 minute), use the QR code, or go to danielplan.com/fitnessmove.

# Praying
## *Together*

Because everything we do in our journey toward health depends on God's power, we end each meeting with prayer and encourage group members to pray for each other during the week.

> *"Rejoice always, pray continually, give thanks in all cir-*
> *cumstances; for this is God's will for you in Christ Jesus."*
> 1 Thessalonians 5:16–18

This week, offer a prayer of gratitude to God. Thank him for friends in your group and outside the group who support your efforts to be healthy. Let group members pray one- or two-sentence prayers of gratitude for friends.

Pray also for those in your group who shared an area of weakness or need. Ask God to strengthen them and surround them with his love, and ask him if there is anything you can do to support them. You can pray as simply as, "Lord, thank you for [*Name*]. Please give him/her _____."

Have someone close with this prayer:

> *Thank you, Lord, for this group and for all of our friends. We long to*
> *become people who love you with all our hearts and who love each other*
> *as you have loved us. We long to learn how to love our neighbors as we*
> *love ourselves. Help us to become people who love more deeply, more*
> *genuinely. Give us the courage to open up to others and be vulnerable.*
> *Give us the patience and care for others that will make us good listeners.*
> *Make us people others can trust with their areas of need. Thank you for*
> *what you are doing in our group. I pray this in Jesus' name. Amen.*

# Honesty: The Real Deal

> "Speaking the truth in love,
> we will grow to become in every
> respect the mature body of him
> who is the head, that is, Christ."
> Ephesians 4:15

We need friendships where we can be vulnerable without fear of judgment or humiliation. We need friends who give us grace: listening, suffering with us, caring for us in our brokenness. We need to be that kind of friend to others. We also need friends who go a step further, who are honest with us when they see us going astray, who can take it when we are graciously honest with them about things they do that hurt us. Honesty like that is a delicate art, and in this session we'll explore that art of grace-filled honesty.

# COMING
# TOGETHER

The other members of your group can be a huge source of support in sustaining healthy changes in your life. Before watching the video, check in with each other about your experiences since the last session. For example:

» Briefly share what Next Steps from Session 1 you completed or tried to complete. Were they helpful? If so, how?

» How did Session 1 affect your relationship with God? With other people?

» Have you been practicing The Daniel Plan in other areas, such as Food or Fitness? If so, what have you done? What is working well for you? What questions do you have? What encouragement do you need?

# LEARNING
# TOGETHER

## AN INTERVIEW WITH **Dr. John Townsend**

Play the video segment for Session 2. As you watch, use the outline provided to follow along or to take additional notes on anything that stands out to you.

» God loves us just as we are, but he also loves us enough to want us not to stay the way we are. He is honest with us about areas where we need to grow.

» There are times when real friends need to be honest with each other about areas where they need to grow.

» Honesty gives a person power, correction, and a path to go on. It is more useful than, "I care about you; I love you; I don't have anything else to say to you."

» We have to be able to receive honesty and to give honesty. It can be in the form of feedback. It can be an encouragement, like "Here's a Bible verse that encouraged me." Or it could be in the form of, "I want to tell you I'm concerned about you."

» When you love someone and treat them with grace, you build up relational equity like money in a bank by earning the person's trust over time. Then when you've earned the trust, you have the right to be honest about something difficult.

» When you can receive honesty about something difficult and not feel bad—not feel shame, not feel rejected—it strengthens you.

» Keeping current and not stuffing down resentment ultimately can bring intimacy. It can bring forgiveness where forgiveness is needed, and thereby bring closeness and connection.

» If you hold on to hurts and are not honest with people, you may tend to stuff down food as well.

» In the military, soldiers ask their superiors, "Do I have permission to speak freely?" PTSF. We need to give each other PTSF.

» If you need to be honest with someone about something difficult, start by being vulnerable. You can say, "If my life is ever going down a cliff, you can tell me about it. Do you love me enough to tell me about it?"

   The other person will say, "Well, sure."

   Then you say, "And if I see you going down a cliff?"

   The person will say, "Well, sure."

   After front-loading the conversation like that, you can say, "Well, let me tell you what is going on."

   Then once again you begin with vulnerability: "I love our friendship and I love how safe we are, but I kind of felt missed when I got a lot of advice from you."

   People can take honesty when you are vulnerable with it. If you come off as a parent saying, "Look, three times you've done this, stop that," it disengages people. Start off with your own need.

» Or you can begin by saying, "You are important, and we're not as good as we need to be, and I miss how good things could be. I'd like for you to back off from the criticism, or give me more space, or show up to meetings on time, or whatever."

> *"The Word became flesh and made his dwelling among us. We have seen his glory, the glory of the one and only Son, who came from the Father, full of grace and truth."*
>
> John 1:14

» Jesus came with grace and truth. The sequence is important. It doesn't say truth and grace. Treating someone with grace over a period of time is what earns us the right to speak truth to them. We treat them with grace by listening, suffering with them, and identifying with them. We send the message, "I'm on your side. Tell me more."

» Timing is important too. When somebody is open about a loss, a failure, something they are humiliated about, that is not the time to confront. They are raw. They need support, love, comfort, and empathy. Difficult truth may have to come in another meeting.

» We need to be honest about the roots and the soil of an issue, not just the fruit. We might say, "I missed you. You're not in a relationship. You went under the radar. Where are you? I want to engage with you."

» People who understand that life doesn't always go as it's supposed to go, that there will be mess-ups and mistakes, are living in reality. But people who feel a demand to have it together, to always live in the victory, are living in delusion. The Bible is a messy book.

» Fragilizing is when we walk on eggshells around other people, not telling them how we feel, not opening up, not telling the truth, because we are afraid we'll hurt them. We treat them as if they are fragile. Fragilizing creates weak friends and weak community. Grown-ups can handle the truth.

» Boundaries are the property lines in a relationship. Sometimes we need to set boundaries with words: "Can you come to our meeting on time?" Or, "Can you not talk about yourself the whole time?" Or, "Can you care about this and not judge me?" Or, "This is hard for me and I'd appreciate it if you did it differently."

» With some people, boundaries have to move from words to actions. Sometimes we have to say, "As long as this behavior stays this way, I've got to spend a little less time with you. I don't want that to happen. I want a full-fledged open relationship. But it's hard to be around you when this happens."

» Grace and truth are the two tracks of a relationship that the train needs to run on.

# GROWING
# TOGETHER

Discuss what you learned from the video. Don't feel obliged to answer every question. Select those that most resonate with your group.

 **1** Would you want someone to tell you the truth if they saw you acting in an unloving manner? If so, how would you want them to go about it? If not, why not?

 **2** How would someone earn the right to tell you difficult truths?

*"Do not rebuke mockers or they will hate you;*
*rebuke the wise and they will love you."*
Proverbs 9:8

What does it mean to have grace in a relationship? What are some ways we can treat people with grace?

 Why is it important to treat someone with grace over a period of time before we start telling them truths that are hard to hear?

 Give an example of what truth with grace sounds like. Give another example of what truth without grace sounds like.

*"'In your anger do not sin': Do not let the sun go down while you are still angry."*

Ephesians 4:26

How would you decide when it's best to shrug off something a friend does and when it's best to be honest with them about how it affected you?

 How do you respond to this statement: "People who feel a demand to have it together, to always live in the victory, are living in delusion. The Bible is a messy book."

# What I Want
## to Remember

Complete this activity on your own.

» Briefly review the video outline and any notes you took. Review also any notes from the discussion.

» In the space below, write down the most significant thing you gained from this session — from the video or the discussion. You can share it with the group if you wish.

# BETTER
# TOGETHER

Now that you've talked about some great ideas, let's get practical — and put what you're learning into action. Begin by identifying one or two steps you can take with what you've explored in this session. Then check out the Food Tip of the Week and the Fitness Move of the Week for some fresh ideas to enrich your journey toward health in those areas. Use or adapt whatever is helpful to you!

# FRIENDS
## *Next Steps*

Here are a few suggested activities to help you develop honesty in your relationships. Check one or two boxes next to the options you'd like to try this week—choose what works for you.

- ☐ Talk with a friend about what you've learned in this session. Tell them you would want them to let you know if they saw you heading in an unhelpful direction. Ask them if they would want you to let them know the same.

- ☐ Spend time with a friend and consciously look for ways to earn their trust. Find ways to practice grace: listening, rejoicing with their joy or mourning with their sorrow (Romans 12:15), being fully present. Give them all the airtime they need. If and when it's your turn to talk about what is on your mind, choose to be vulnerable. Don't try to look as if you have it all together.

- ☐ Make plans to attend a worship service with one or more people you want to be friends with. If your small group doesn't worship at the same service, take the lead in seeing how many group members can do so.

- ☐ Look for someone at work who might want to be an ally with you in living a healthy lifestyle. Invite that person to go for a walk with you or share a lunch.

☐ Is there someone you need to be honest with about something difficult? If so, have you earned their trust enough to do that? If you haven't always treated them with grace, maybe the first step is asking for their forgiveness for your side of the relationship.

☐ If you need to be honest with someone and asking for their forgiveness isn't an issue, then choose a time when they are in a strong frame of mind to hear you. Don't choose a time when they are raw and in need of encouragement. Begin by conveying how much you value your friendship. Approach the person with vulnerability, not a desire to get back at them. If you're angry, take your anger to God and vent it to him first, so that you don't vent it unhelpfully at the person.

☐ Do you feel that you have no one in your life with whom you can be honest? Read "Choosing Safe People" in the Appendix. Who do you know that fits the profile of a safe person? Take a step to get to know that person better. And make a point of learning to be a safe person yourself.

# Food Tip
## *of the Week*

Food and friends—it's what so many of life's memorable moments are based upon. And the results are definitely better when we do it together. Through teamwork we win! For your next gathering, try this delicious recipe for avocado ceviche with fresh herbs, vegetables, and bright citrus flavors. Just click the Food Tip of the Week on your video screen (3 minutes), scan the QR code, or go to danielplan.com/foodtip. You'll also find this recipe in *The Daniel Plan Cookbook*.

# Fitness Move
## *of the Week*

This week's move is a workout for both body and brain. It will help you build your coordination and memory. Just click the Fitness Move of the Week on your video screen (1 minute), use the QR code, or go to danielplan.com/fitnessmove.

# Praying
## *Together*

Because everything we do in our journey toward health depends on God's power, we end each meeting with prayer and encourage group members to pray for each other during the week.

> *"I can do everything through Christ,*
> *who gives me strength."*
> Philippians 4:13 (NLT)

Get into smaller groups of two or three people. Tell your partner(s) how you would like them to pray for you. What is one thing you need? Don't shift attention to the needs of someone outside the group—share your own need. It might be some area of growth related to The Daniel Plan, or it might be something else. When each person has shared, pray for your partner(s). Two sentences of prayer are enough if you are new to praying aloud with others.

After you've prayed in smaller groups, have someone close with this prayer:

> *Father, we want to earn the right to be honest with our friends. We want to be people others can trust. Please help us with that, and show us anything we do that keeps others from trusting us. We don't want to walk on eggshells with people. We want to relate as grown-ups to grown-ups. Please help us be people of grace, listening intently to others and rejoicing or suffering with them. Please help us speak truth with love and humility. I pray this in Jesus' name. Amen.*

# Moving through Grief and Loss

> "Blessed are those who mourn,
> for they will be comforted."
> Matthew 5:4

We prefer not to think about them, but loss and failure happen to all of us sooner or later. And when significant loss or failure occurs, we're not designed to shrug it off and keep moving. We're designed to grieve. If we don't grieve, our physical or mental health suffers, or pieces of our souls turn to ice. So grieving, it turns out, is a crucial part of growing through challenging times.

We need other people to help us grieve effectively. God made us in such a way that we actually can't grieve all by ourselves. Our instinct may be to withdraw when we're sad, but with significant losses, we need the involvement of friends. In this session, we'll explore how the grief process works and the role that friends play in it.

# COMING
# TOGETHER

---

The other members of your group can be a huge source of support in sustaining healthy changes in your life. Before watching the video, check in with each other about your experiences since the last session. For example:

» Briefly share what Next Steps from Session 2 you completed or tried to complete. Were they helpful? If so, how?

» How did Session 2 affect your relationship with God? With other people?

» Have you been practicing The Daniel Plan in other areas, such as Food or Fitness? If so, what have you done? What is working well for you? What questions do you have? What encouragement do you need?

# LEARNING
# TOGETHER

Play the video segment for Session 3. As you watch, use the outline provided to follow along or to take additional notes on anything that stands out to you.

> *"He is despised and rejected by men, a Man of sorrows and acquainted with grief."*
> Isaiah 53:3 (NKJV)

» Grief is a skill; there are things we need to know how to do. Community is essential for learning how to grieve well. We need to be with people who care about us and take us through the grieving process.

» **Step 1** in grieving is accepting that there was a loss or a failure. The alternative is to minimize the event, to say it wasn't that bad. But if we minimize how bad things really are, we never heal how bad things really are.

» We can't accept the loss by ourselves. We tend to shy away from it, not think about it, get busy. But community comes in and says, "I want to know. Let's talk about it."

» The harder and deeper the loss, or the more devastating the failure, the more grace is required in order to accept it. That grace comes from God through other people. We need somebody to be present, to give us support and validation, to say, "Tell me more about it." As we feel their love, we are able to look more and more at what really happened.

» **Step 2** in grieving is to receive comfort. When a loss or a failure can't be fixed, we just need comfort for the pain. We need someone to be with us, to say, "Tell me more," "How does that feel?" and sometimes even, "What you're going through must be horrific." At other times we need someone to say nothing at all.

*"Now when Job's three friends heard of all this adversity that had come upon him, each one came from his own place . . . [to] mourn with him, and to comfort him . . . So they sat down with him on the ground seven days and seven nights, and no one spoke a word to him, for they saw that his grief was very great."*

Job 2:11 – 13 (NKJV)

» **Step 3** is the actual grieving. It is letting go, saying goodbye, saying "I can't keep you. You've left me."

» The function of grief is to reset the buttons so we can move on, learn lessons, and be better. If we can't grieve, then we still have arguments in our heads: Why did that happen? Where was God at that time? We lose energy, focus, goals. Grief says, "I've got to empty it all out so that I'll feel better and then I can move on."

» Grief is a physical thing where we actually let out how much we cared about the person or thing. We do something physical like crying.

*"God is our merciful Father and the source of all comfort. He comforts us in all our troubles so that we can comfort others. When they are troubled, we will be able to give them the same comfort God has given us."*

2 Corinthians 1:3 – 4 (NLT)

» God made us so that when we have an experience, it goes down our neuropathways from our present brain into the storage system of lessons and memories. But when we are overwhelmed with a loss we can't deal with, the neuropathway gets cut off, like a traffic jam. The experience continues to feel like it's here and now. When that happens, we need to talk about the experience with people who listen attentively and give us eye contact, people who will draw us out and help us cry. Eventually the traffic jam will loosen up, and the experience will become just a memory. It no longer feels like it's here and now.

» **Step 4** is restoration. God doesn't give us back the same person or job, but he restores us with other relationships, another job.

> *"I will restore to you the years that the
> swarming locust has eaten."*
> Joel 2:25 (NKJV)

» **Step 5** is adaptation. We learn to do a relationship in a different way or to make a living in a different way. We adapt to the new normal.

» We need to make grief a positive thing so we can get the power from it. We need to ask people, "Is that sad for you?" We need to tell people when we are sad instead of saying, "It's not that bad; I've got the victory." We need to be honest and allow the comfort and transformation to happen.

» We need to allow grief to come in waves. It comes in and we feel it intensely and might have to call a friend for comfort or prayer, then it subsides, and then it comes back. But if we pay attention to it and don't fight it and do all five steps, it does resolve. Grief is a season that doesn't last forever.

# GROWING
# TOGETHER

Discuss what you learned from the video. Don't feel obliged to answer every question. Select those that most resonate with your group.

**1** How comfortable are you with the idea of talking to other people about your losses or failures? Why?

**2** What has been a significant loss you have faced in your life?

*"Rejoice with those who rejoice;*
*mourn with those who mourn."*

Romans 12:15

What would you want other people to do if you had a significant loss or failure? What would communicate comfort to you?

 What does it take to say, "Goodbye. I can't keep you. You've left me"? Why is that so overwhelming to say before we're ready?

 What role can other people play as we seek to get to the point where we can say goodbye?

 Is there any loss that you haven't fully grieved all the way to Step 5? If so, at which step do you think you are currently? And how can the group support you?

**7** As Matthew 26:36–38 illustrates, even Jesus wanted his closest friends with him when he was grieving. Why is that important to know?

> *"Then Jesus went with his disciples to a place called Gethsemane, and he said to them, 'Sit here while I go over there and pray.' He took Peter and the two sons of Zebedee along with him, and he began to be sorrowful and troubled. Then he said to them, 'My soul is overwhelmed with sorrow to the point of death. Stay here and keep watch with me.'"*
>
> Matthew 26:36–38

# What I Want
## to Remember

Complete this activity on your own.

» Briefly review the video outline and any notes you took. Review also any notes from the discussion.

» In the space below, write down the most significant thing you gained from this session—from the video or the discussion. You can share it with the group if you wish.

# BETTER
# TOGETHER

Now that you've talked about some great ideas, let's get practical—and put what you're learning into action. Begin by identifying one or two steps you can take with what you've explored in this session. Then check out the Food Tip of the Week and the Fitness Move of the Week for some fresh ideas to enrich your journey toward health in those areas. Use or adapt whatever is helpful to you!

# FRIENDS
## Next Steps

Here are a few suggested activities to help you develop the skill of grieving. Check one or two boxes next to the options you'd like to try this week—choose what works for you.

☐ Write a list of the biggest losses you have suffered in your life. Include losses in childhood, especially if a parent died, if your parents divorced, or if one or both parents gave you significantly less nurture than you needed. Include job losses that weren't your choice, broken relationships that significantly affected you, and times when you failed at something that mattered to you. When you've made your list, put a check mark beside those items that you think you are truly over—you've grieved them enough, and you've experienced restoration. Circle any items that you have minimized or that you haven't fully let go of. About which ones are you still asking, "Why did God allow that?"

☐ Talk with a friend about an unresolved loss or failure. Tell them what happened and how it still affects you. Are you sad? Angry? Ashamed? Do you feel nothing, but you have behaviors such as nightmares or binge eating? If you think you know at which step of the grieving process you are, tell your friend that. If your friend is inclined to problem solve or "cheer you up," tell them that what you really need is eye contact, listening, and emotional engagement. Try to choose a friend who is able to feel with others rather than simply analyze. On the other hand, if what comforts you most is person-to-person presence without a lot of emoting, that's okay.

☐ Listen to a friend who needs to talk about a loss or failure. Give eye contact. Listen closely and ask questions that invite your friend to go as deep as they want. Try to tune in to what they are feeling and respond accordingly. Avoid giving advice or pushing them to get over it.

☐ If you feel stuck on a loss that is causing major symptoms (depression, anxiety, insomnia, panic attacks, etc.) that don't get under control when you talk with a friend, consider talking with a professional counselor who is trained to help you through the grief process.

☐ If you have no losses that need to be addressed, make plans to get together with a friend and give them encouragement, support, and a listening ear.

# Food Tip
## *of the Week*

Can you imagine comfort food that is completely healthy and tastes great? Check out this recipe for turkey chili, and learn about other great comfort food recipes like macaroni and cheese, meatloaf, and chicken noodle soup in *The Daniel Plan Cookbook*. Just click the Food Tip of the Week on your video screen (3 minutes), scan the QR code, or go to danielplan. com/foodtip.

# Fitness Move
## *of the Week*

This week's move uses an exercise band to work on all parts of your body, especially glutes, quads, and shoulders. Just click the Fitness Move of the Week on your video screen (1 minute), use the QR code, or go to danielplan. com/fitnessmove.

# Praying
## Together

Because everything we do in our journey toward health depends on God's power, we end each meeting with prayer and encourage group members to pray for each other during the week.

> *"Have mercy on me, LORD, for I am faint; heal me,*
> *LORD, for my bones are in agony."*
> Psalm 6:2

Get into smaller groups of two or three people. If you have a loss you'd like prayer for, share that with your partner(s). If not, tell your partner(s) one thing you personally need from God. This is not a prayer request for someone else, but a request for you. What do you need from God? Power to follow through on some aspect of The Daniel Plan? Wisdom and guidance about a decision? Encouragement? A deeper awareness of God's love? Name at least one thing you need from God. Then pray for one another about the needs you've shared.

After you've prayed in smaller groups, have someone close with this prayer:

*Lord, your Holy Spirit is the Comforter. He is the One who comes alongside us to help us do what we can't do on our own and the One who binds up our wounds when we're grieving. Please fill us with your Holy Spirit so that we can be comforted in the areas of our losses. If we've suffered a loss, please help us stop any minimizing we might be doing and accept that we've lost something precious. Please give us the courage to talk with someone, to cry, to let the grief out of our bodies. Please also fill us with your Spirit to be your comforting presence with others. Please show us who to listen to, to hug, to cry with. We want to comfort others with the comfort we've received from you. Thank you for the comfort you have given and will continue to give us, and thank you for the people in this group. I pray this in Jesus' name. Amen.*

# God's Purpose for Living

"For we are God's handiwork, created in Christ Jesus to do good works, which God prepared in advance for us to do."
Ephesians 2:10

Community can help us get through hard things and make healthy changes in our lives. It can also do something more: it can help us identify what God has given us to do in the world in this season of our lives. We may not have one mission for our whole life, and we don't need to know what God plans for us to do twenty years from now. What we need to know is: What does God want of me in this season? How has God shaped me in order to contribute to his world here and now? We don't have to figure this out in isolation. In this session, we'll look at some ways community can help us identify our passion, meaning, and skills.

# COMING
# TOGETHER

The other members of your group can be a huge source of support in sustaining healthy changes in your life. Before watching the video, check in with each other about your experiences since the last session. For example:

» Briefly share what Next Steps from Session 3 you completed or tried to complete. Were they helpful? If so, how?

» How did Session 3 affect your relationship with God? With other people?

» Have you been practicing The Daniel Plan in other areas, such as Food or Fitness? If so, what have you done? What is working well for you? What questions do you have? What encouragement do you need?

# LEARNING
# TOGETHER

Play the video segment for Session 4. As you watch, use the outline provided to follow along or to take additional notes on anything that stands out to you.

» Recovery and health aren't ends in themselves. We recover and get healthy *so that* we can glorify God with our lives. We need to find out what mission God has given us.

» Here are three practical factors in finding our mission:

  • Passion

  • Meaning

  • Skills

» First, God meant us to have passion. We are supposed to feel things. We know we have passion when we lose track of time while doing something.

» Passion helps us move ahead, have energy, and persevere through conflicts.

» Passion rises up when we are able to move out of survival mode.

» At a very high rate, people regret what they did not do much more than they regret what they did do.

» Friends can help each other identify their passions by paying attention and saying, "You seem passionate when you _____."

» Second, God wants our lives to have meaning. When passion is all about us, it lacks meaning and is ultimately empty and unsatisfying. We have passion with meaning when our passion is about God, not about us.

» The happiest people in the world are the ones who know that when they finish their time on earth, the world will be a better place, the kingdom of God will have been expanded, and good will be winning over evil. That's what meaning is about. It's, "How do I fit in the army of God, in God's big picture?"

» People in community can help each other identify the meaning that fits with their passion. They can take the trouble to think about how God has made their friend. They can ponder the possibilities. "Maybe you could use that passion to serve God by _____."

» Unless we are in a big crisis, we should find some area where we can serve others even while we are healing ourselves. Instead of sitting at home and trying to think of something we are passionate about, we should try volunteering in some service organization that our church can connect us with. Experience is a great way to identify a meaningful passion.

» Helping other people stimulates the brain chemicals that make us feel happy.

» When we find something we're passionate about, we may need to get training, coaching, or mentoring to develop the skills we need to serve in that arena. What are our strengths that need to be developed and used?

» There are tools like *Strengthsfinder*™ available that can help us identify our strengths.

» Friends can help each other recognize their strengths and skills, which they can use to serve others. "I have noticed that you are good at _____."

# GROWING
# TOGETHER

Discuss what you learned from the video. Don't feel obliged to answer every question. Select those that most resonate with your group.

 What are you passionate about? Do you know?

 What indications of passion have you seen in other members of your group? How would you complete this sentence about other group members: "You seem passionate when you _____." (Or, "One of your strengths is _____.")

 What is meaning? Why is it important to have meaning connected to our passion? Consider the following Scriptures as you answer.

*"I urge you to live a life worthy of the calling you have received."*

Ephesians 4:1

*"Now to each one the manifestation of the*
*Spirit is given for the common good."*
1 Corinthians 12:7

If you have a passion but don't know how it serves God or makes the world a better place, offer it to the group and invite their input: "Maybe you could use that passion to serve God by _____."

*"Then the righteous will answer him, 'Lord, when did*
*we see you hungry and feed you, or thirsty and give you*
*something to drink? When did we see you a stranger and*
*invite you in, or needing clothes and clothe you? When*
*did we see you sick or in prison and go to visit you?'*

*"The King will reply, 'Truly I tell you, whatever*
*you did for one of the least of these brothers*
*and sisters of mine, you did for me.'"*
Matthew 25:37–40

What opportunities for serving others does your church or community offer? If you don't know, how could you find out?

If you're busy raising a family, how can you find mission in the activities you are already committed to? For instance, how can you involve your kids in serving their sports team members? How can you be of service to other parents, such as the parents of your children's teammates? Or how can you involve your kids in an outreach to the poor in your community?

 What are the most valuable things you have gotten out of this study of Friends? What will you take with you?

# What I Want
## *to Remember*

Complete this activity on your own.

» Briefly review the video outline and any notes you took. Review also any notes from the discussion.

» In the space below, write down the most significant thing you gained from this session—from the video or the discussion. You can share it with the group if you wish.

# BETTER
# TOGETHER

Now that you've talked about some great ideas, let's get practical — and put what you're learning into action. Begin by identifying one or two steps you can take with what you've explored in this session. Then check out the Food Tip of the Week and the Fitness Move of the Week for some fresh ideas to enrich your journey toward health in those areas. Use or adapt whatever is helpful to you!

# FRIENDS
## *Next Steps*

Here are a few suggested activities to help you move forward in living out your mission. Check one or two boxes next to the options you'd like to try this week — choose what works for you.

☐ Get together with a friend to talk about where each of you fits in God's purposes. What is your passion? What passion do you see in your friend? How could your passion make the world a better place? What strengths does your friend have? What strengths does your friend see in you? What skills do each of you need to develop? If you don't know what your passion is, in what areas of service could you experiment? Reflect back to your friend what you see in him or her, and encourage one another to take a step forward.

☐ Take an inventory like *Strengthsfinder*™ to identify your talents and abilities. Share the results with a friend. Does your friend confirm what the inventory says? What might you do with the strengths you have identified? Are there any ministries or areas of service that fit the way you are designed? How might you develop skills that are already present in you?

☐ Do some research about the ministries that help your church run, as well as outreach opportunities to those in need. How can you contribute to the things that need to get done in your church or your community? Take the results of your research back to your small group.

☐ Involve your children in an outreach to the needy in your community or around the world. Children can help raise funds, or join you in shopping for food for a food bank or socks for the homeless. Or you can sponsor a child and involve your kids in learning about the country where the sponsored child lives. Involving your children like this contributes to your mission as a parent, because it helps you raise them to care about serving others.

# Food Tip
## of the Week

Teaching the kids in your life to eat healthily will influence them their entire lives. Get them cooking with you, involved in the kitchen, and they will be more likely to try new foods. Learn terrific tips for cooking with kids and a recipe for healthy chicken nuggets. Click the Food Tip of the Week on your video screen (3 minutes), scan the QR code, or go to danielplan.com/foodtip.

# Fitness Move
## of the Week

This week's move is a workout for both body and brain. It will help you build your coordination and memory. Just click the Fitness Move of the Week on your video screen (1 minute), use the QR code, or go to danielplan.com/fitnessmove.

# Praying
## *Together*

Because everything we do in our journey toward health depends on God's power, we end each meeting with prayer and encourage group members to pray for each other during the week.

> *"Enter his gates with thanksgiving and his courts with praise; give thanks to him and praise his name."*
> Psalm 100:4

Let each person pray for the person on his or her right. Pray a prayer of thanks and blessing for that person. Thank God for the passion he has given that person. Thank him for the unique way he has designed that person to serve him. Thank him for that person's skills. If you know some of that person's strengths, thank God for those specifically. Or if the person has contributed to your group in some way, thank God for that.

Have someone close with this prayer:

*Father, you have given each of us the unique power of the Holy Spirit to serve the common good—the good of our whole group, the good of our families, the good of our church and community. Please show each of us how you have designed us to serve you. Please let our passion well up from inside us so that we can see it and others can see it. Please help us find ways to practice our passion that are all about you, not about us. Thank you for the friendships that have been forming here, and for the opportunities you've given us to be friends to each other. Please show us how to cultivate those friendships as we go forward. I pray this in Jesus' name. Amen.*

# Appendix

# If It's Hard for You to Be Vulnerable

If the very idea of being vulnerable with someone about your need or weakness makes you want to scream, laugh, or hide, you have a barrier to overcome. What might that barrier be? It's probably shame.

Shame is the fear of exposure. It's the feeling that if we are seen and known for who we really are, something bad will happen. It usually has its roots in past experiences. In the past, we *were* seen and something bad happened! For instance, we behaved badly as children, and our parents somehow sent the message not that the behavior was unacceptable but that *we* were unacceptable. We made honest mistakes as children (accidentally spilling a glass of milk, for example) and were punished as if the mistake were deliberate. Or we were ridiculed for our mistakes or perceived flaws: "He's my clumsy child." "She'll never be pretty, poor thing." The punishment or ridicule may have come from parents, teachers, schoolmates — anyone whose opinion mattered to us.

Shame is hardest to overcome when it has roots in childhood, because those are the deepest roots of all. Suppose you say to a potential friend, "Sometimes I struggle with _____." That potential friend might raise his eyebrows and change the subject. If you're not burdened by shame, you may conclude, "This person isn't someone I can trust." Or possibly, "This must not be a good time for him to listen to my personal life. I wonder what's going on in his life?" But if you're burdened by shame, you may conclude, "I just made an idiot of myself. He must think I'm a loser. I'm never doing that again." The rejection feels like it exposes the raw, tender part of your soul that has been hurt in the past.

One way to combat shame is with the truth of Scripture. The apostle Paul says, "There is now no condemnation for those who are in Christ Jesus" (Romans 8:1). No condemnation! He goes on to say,

*"If God is for us, who can be against us? He who did not spare his own Son, but gave him up for us all—how will he not also, along with him, graciously give us all things? Who will bring any charge against those whom God has chosen? It is God who justifies. Who then is the one who condemns? No one. Christ Jesus who died—more than that, who was raised to life—is at the right hand of God and is also interceding for us."*

Romans 8:31–34

Who can be against us? No one whose opinion truly matters. Who can truly condemn us? No one. Jesus Christ is standing for us right now in the Father's presence.

The psalmist says to God, "No one who hopes in you will ever be put to shame" (Psalm 25:3). If we put our hope in God, shame has no hold over us.

If you struggle with shame, don't conclude that vulnerable relationships aren't for you. Shame may be part of what is driving your unhealthy ways of living, and opening up in trustworthy relationships is the key to healing your shame. Instead of giving up on vulnerability, use good judgment in choosing someone to open up to. Here are some questions you might ask yourself:

» *Is this person available?* If she's too busy, she may not be a good fit for you. But don't assume that everyone in the world is too busy for you. That's your shame talking.

» *Does he have the needed expertise?* This question matters if you need to talk with someone about something specialized, such as a problem at work. If the person needs to understand the technicalities of your job in order to give you helpful feedback, look for someone who qualifies. But don't underestimate the potential of a caring outsider if solving the technicalities isn't your real need.

» *Is this person a peer?* Someone in a leadership role over you might be able to offer wisdom and guidance, but that person may not have the potential to be a friend. Subordinates probably don't either. Look for someone with whom you can give and receive. Friendship is about mutuality.

» *What is this person's reputation?* If others mistrust him, maybe you should too. But if others trust him, maybe you can too.

» *Is this person a good listener?* Do you feel like this person is emotionally present with others? Or does she lose eye contact or constantly check her phone for texts?

» *Is this a considerate person?* Avoid those who are harsh or who tend to minimize issues by saying things like, "Oh, you'll be fine."

» *Is there a potential for continuity in this relationship?* Friendships rarely become deeply vulnerable right away. They build over time. Look for someone you can see regularly. That way, if you open up about an issue today, you can revisit it next month if need be.

» *Are my expectations reasonable?* Some expectations that can get you into trouble are, "If I share this issue, he will completely agree with me" and "If I open up to her, she will open up to me, too, right away." Also, while you want the potential for continuity, a person who agrees to have lunch with you isn't thereby obligated to have lunch with you every week.

Don't let shame keep you isolated! Maybe there's someone in your small group to whom you could admit, "Sometimes I struggle with shame."

# Choosing Safe People

If you have a pattern of getting deeply wounded in relationships, it could be that you are choosing to get close to unsafe people. Part of developing healthy community is learning to identify and choose safe people. Here are some of the qualities to look for:

» Safe people admit their weaknesses. They don't pretend to have their lives perfectly together.

» Safe people are open to feedback. They don't get defensive when you graciously tell them something about them that troubles you. (Of course, the assumption here is that you are doing it graciously, not with a critical or superior spirit.)

» Safe people take responsibility for their errors. They don't blame others.

» When they find out they have done something that hurts others, safe people change their behavior. They don't just apologize and continue the bad behavior. Of course, they're not perfect, so they may make the same mistake again, but they genuinely work on their character flaws and try to change. They don't avoid the subject and make excuses.

» Safe people are willing to earn other people's trust. They don't demand trust without evidence of good character.

» Safe people tell the truth.

» Safe people let others get to know the real them.

» Safe people are interested in getting to know the real you.

» Safe people are empathic. They try to put themselves in other people's shoes, see things from their point of view, understand how they feel and think. They don't lose track of their own feelings and opinions, but they are not so rigidly attached to their feelings and opinions that they are blind to alternatives.

» Safe people see other people's pain and want to help.

» Safe people take "no" for an answer. When others say "no," they don't withdraw emotionally or inflict guilt.

» Safe people allow appropriate separateness in a relationship. They have their own lives (interests, friends) separate from their friends, and they want their friends to have lives too.

» If you do something wrong, safe people tell you to your face that they are hurt. They tell you respectfully, without venting anger or shame at you. Unsafe people tell others you hurt them, withdraw emotionally, or use shame when they let you know they're hurt.

» When you do something wrong and genuinely apologize, safe people forgive you. Unsafe people continue to hold it against you.

Lots of safe people are out there! If you have trouble finding safe people to be close to, see the book *Safe People: How to Find Relationships That Are Good for You and Avoid Those That Aren't* by Henry Cloud and John Townsend.

# Group Guidelines

Our goal: To provide a safe environment where participants experience authentic community and spiritual growth.

| OUR VALUES | |
|---|---|
| **Group Attendance** | To give priority to the group meeting. We will call or email if we will be late or absent. |
| **Safe Environment** | To help create a safe place where people can be heard and feel loved. |
| **Respect Differences** | To be gentle and gracious to people with different spiritual maturity, personal opinions, or personalities. Remember we are all works in progress! |
| **Confidentiality** | To keep anything that is shared strictly confidential and within the group, and to avoid sharing information about those outside the group. |
| **Encouragement for Growth** | We want to spiritually multiply our life by serving others with our God-given gifts. |
| **Rotating Hosts/Leaders and Homes** | To encourage different people to host the group in their homes, and to rotate the responsibility of facilitating each meeting. |

We have found that groups thrive when they talk about expectations up front and come into agreement on some of these details listed below.

Refreshments/mealtimes _____

Child care _____

When we will meet (day of week) _____

Where we will meet (place) _____

We will begin at (time) _____ and end at _____

We will look for a compatible time to attend a worship service together.

Our primary worship service time will be _____

# Leadership 101

**Congratulations!** You have responded to the call to help shepherd Jesus' flock. There are few other tasks in the family of God that surpass the contribution you will be making. As you prepare to lead, whether it is one session or four, here are a few thoughts to keep in mind. We encourage you to read these and review them with each new discussion leader before he or she leads.

1. **Remember that you are not alone.** God knows everything about you, and he knew that you would be asked to lead your group. It is common for leaders to feel that they are not ready to lead. Moses, Solomon, Jeremiah, Timothy—they all were reluctant to lead. God promises, "Never will I leave you; never will I forsake you" (Hebrews 13:5). You will be blessed as you serve.

2. **Don't try to do it alone.** Pray right now for God to help you build a healthy leadership team. If you can enlist a co-leader to help you lead the group, you will find your experience to be much richer. That person might take half the group in a second discussion circle if your group is as large as ten people or more. Your co-leader might lead the prayer time or handle the hosting tasks, welcoming people and getting them refreshments. This is your chance to involve as many people as you can in building a healthy group. All you have to do is call and ask people to help; you'll be surprised at the response.

3. **Just be yourself.** God wants you to use your unique gifts and temperament. Don't try to do things exactly like another leader; do them in a way that fits you! Just admit it when you don't have an answer, and apologize when you make a mistake. Your group will love you for it, and you'll sleep better at night.

4.  **Prepare for your meeting ahead of time.** Review the session, view the video, and write down your responses to each question. If paper and pens are needed, such as for gathering group members' names and email addresses (see "Coming Together" in Session 1), be sure you have the necessary supplies. Think about which "Next Steps" you will do.

    If you're leading Session 1, look over the Group Guidelines and be ready to review them with the group. If child care will be an issue for your group, for example, be prepared to talk about options. Some groups have the adults share the cost of a babysitter (or two) to care for children in a different part of the house where the adults are meeting. Other groups use one home for the kids and another for the adults. A third idea is to rotate the responsibility of caring for the children in the same home or one nearby.

5.  **Pray for your group members by name.** Before you begin your session, go around the room in your mind and pray for each member. You may want to review the group's prayer list at least once a week. Ask God to use your time together to work in the heart of each person uniquely. Expect God to lead you to whomever he wants you to encourage or challenge in a special way.

6.  **When you ask a question, be patient.** Read each question aloud and wait for someone to respond. Sometimes people need a moment or two of silence to think about the question, and if silence doesn't bother you, it won't bother anyone else. After someone responds, affirm the response with a simple "thanks" or "good job." Then ask, "How about somebody else?" or "Would someone who hasn't shared like to add anything?" Be sensitive to new people or reluctant members who aren't ready to participate yet. If you give them a safe setting, they will open up over time. Don't go around the circle and have everyone answer every question. Your goal is a conversation in which the group members talk to each other in a natural way.

7. **Break up into small groups each week or people won't stay.** If your group has more than eight people, we strongly encourage you to have the group gather sometimes in discussion circles of three or four people during the "Growing Together" section of the study. With a greater opportunity to talk in a small circle, people will connect more with the study, apply more quickly what they are learning, and ultimately get more out of it. A small circle also encourages a quiet person to participate and tends to minimize the effect of a more vocal or dominant member. It can also help people feel more loved in your group. When you gather again at the end of the section, you can have one person summarize the highlights from each circle.

   **Small circles are also helpful during prayer time.** People who are not accustomed to praying aloud will feel more comfortable trying it with just two or three others. Also, prayer requests won't take as much time, so circles will have more time to actually pray. When you gather back with the whole group, you can have one person from each circle briefly update everyone on the prayer requests.

8. **One final challenge for new leaders:** Before your opportunity to lead, look up each of the four passages listed below. Read each one as a devotional exercise to help equip you with a shepherd's heart. If you do this, you will be more than ready for your first meeting.

   Matthew 9:36
   1 Peter 5:2 – 4
   Psalm 23
   Ezekiel 34:11 – 16

For additional tips and resources, go to danielplan.com/tools.

# Memory Verses

## SESSION 1

"Carry each other's burdens, and in this way you will fulfill the law of Christ."

*Galatians 6:2*

## SESSION 2

"Speaking the truth in love, we will grow to become in every respect the mature body of him who is the head, that is, Christ."

*Ephesians 4:15*

## SESSION 3

"Rejoice with those who rejoice; mourn with those who mourn."

*Romans 12:15*

## SESSION 4

"For we are God's handiwork, created in Christ Jesus to do good works, which God prepared in advance for us to do."

*Ephesians 2:10*

# About the Contributors

**Dr. John Townsend** is a *New York Times* bestselling author, business consultant, leadership coach, and psychologist. He has written or cowritten twenty-seven books, including the *Boundaries* series, *Leadership Beyond Reason*, and *Handling Difficult People*. For more than twenty years Dr. Townsend has engaged with leaders, organizations, and individuals around the globe, offering them life-changing solutions to their problems. John is founder of the Townsend Institute for Leadership and Counseling.

**Dee Eastman** is the Founding Director of The Daniel Plan that has helped over 15,000 people lose 260,000 pounds in the first year alone. Dee completed her education in Health Science with an emphasis in long-term lifestyle change. Her experience in corporate wellness and ministry has fueled her passion to help people transform their health while drawing closer to God. She coauthored the *Doing Life Together* Bible study series and was a contributing author of *The Daniel Plan*.

## SIGNATURE CHEFS

**Jenny Ross** is the internationally recognized chef, author, educator, and force behind Jenny Ross Living Foods, including the raw food restaurant 118 Degrees, the popular Raw Basics detox meal programs, and nationwide grocery product line 118 Degrees. She has been an early pioneer of the raw movement, coaching clients about the healing power of living foods, while motivating them to adopt a more vibrant, healthy lifestyle. She has a degree in holistic nutrition and certificates as a health and life coach. Jenny was one of the contributing chefs of *The Daniel Plan Cookbook*.

**Mareya Ibrahim** is best known as "The Fit Foodie." She is an award-winning entrepreneur, television chef, author, and one of The Daniel Plan signature chefs. She is also the CEO and founder of Grow Green Industries, Inc. and cocreator of eatCleaner, the premier lifestyle destination for fit food information. Her book *The Clean Eating Handbook* is touted as the "go-to" guide for anyone looking to eat cleaner and get leaner. She is a featured chef on ABC's Emmy-nominated cooking show *Recipe Rehab*, eHow.com, and Livestrong, and the food expert for San Diego's Channel 6 News.

**Robert Sturm** is one of California's premier chefs and food designers. He has been in the food service industry for more than thirty years, working as an independent consultant to leading restaurant chains around the country. He has been featured in many publications, appears on television and radio, and has been a featured chef at the United Nations, the White House, and the Kremlin. Robert is the three-time winner of the U.S. Chef's Open, a past gold medal member of the U.S. Culinary Olympic Team, and has won many national and international culinary titles and food design awards.

## FITNESS TEAM

**Sean Foy** is an internationally renowned authority on fitness, weight management, and healthy living. As an author, exercise physiologist, behavioral coach, and speaker, Sean has earned the reputation as "America's Fast Fitness Expert." With an upbeat and sensible approach to making fitness happen, he's taken the message of "simple moves" fitness all over the world. Sean is the author of *Fitness That Works, Walking 4 Wellness, The Burst Workout,* and a contributing author *The Daniel Plan*.

**Basheerah Ahmad** is a well-known celebrity fitness expert, with a heart for serving God's people. Whether it be through television appearances (*Dr. Phil, The Doctors*), writing fitness and nutrition books, speaking publicly about health, or teaching classes in under-served communities, Basheerah has dedicated her life to improving the health of people everywhere. She has a MS in Exercise Science and numerous certifications in fitness and nutrition. She was a lead fitness instructor for *The Daniel Plan in Action* fitness video series.

**Tony "The Marine" Lattimore** is one of Southern California's premier fitness experts. A skilled personal trainer who privately trains professional athletes, celebrities, and community leaders, he has competed nationally as a bodybuilder. Tony's fitness expertise was featured in P90X and *The Daniel Plan in Action* fitness video series. His powerhouse workouts have a reputation for making fitness fun and exhilarating.

**Kevin Forbes** has a passion for inspiring others to build healthy habits and push through their physical and mental boundaries. Kevin has helped others grow as a personal trainer, group fitness instructor, and fitness professional. Most recently, he was a featured fitness instructor in *The Daniel Plan in Action* fitness video series. Kevin mentors not only future fitness leaders but also the foster youth in his local community.

**Janet Hertogh** shares her love and enthusiasm for teaching in the classroom as an elementary school teacher and in a variety of fitness classes at Saddleback Church. Her passion for life change and transformation is a central theme wherever she goes. Her Masters Degree in Education along with her AFAA and personal training certification make her fully equipped to influence many. Janet was a featured fitness instructor in *The Daniel Plan in Action* fitness video series.

## The Daniel Plan

### 40 Days to a Healthier Life

*Rick Warren D. Min., Daniel Amen M.D.,*
*Mark Hyman M.D.*

Revolutionize Your Health ... Once and for All.

During an afternoon of baptizing over 800 people, Pastor Rick Warren realized it was time for change. He told his congregation he needed to lose weight and asked if anyone wanted to join him. He thought maybe 200 people would sign up; instead he witnessed a movement unfold as 15,000 people lost over 260,000 pounds in the first year. With assistance from medical and fitness experts, Pastor Rick and thousands of people began a journey to transform their lives.

Welcome to The Daniel Plan.

Here's the secret sauce: The Daniel Plan is designed to be done in a supportive community relying on God's instruction for living.

When it comes to getting healthy, two are always better than one. Our research has revealed that people getting healthy together lose twice as much weight as those who do it alone. God never meant for you to go through life alone and that includes the journey to health.

Unlike the thousands of other books on the market, this book is not about a new diet, guilt-driven gym sessions, or shame-driven fasts. *The Daniel Plan* shows you how the powerful combination of faith, fitness, food, focus, and friends will change your health forever, transforming you in the most head-turning way imaginably — from the inside out.

*Available in stores and online!*

## The Daniel Plan Cookbook

### Healthy Eating for Life

*Rick Warren D. Min., Daniel Amen M.D., and Mark Hyman M.D. featuring The Daniel Plan Signature Chefs*

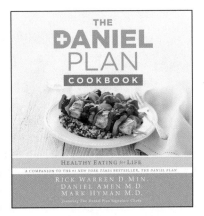

Based on *The Daniel Plan* book, *The Daniel Plan Cookbook: 40 Days to a Healthier Life* is a beautiful four-color cookbook filled with more than 100 delicious, Daniel Plan-approved recipes that offer an abundance of options to bring healthy cooking into your kitchen.

No boring drinks or bland entrées here. Get ready to enjoy appetizing, inviting, clean, simple meals to share in community with your friends and family.

Healthy cooking can be easy and delicious, and *The Daniel Plan Cookbook* is the mouth-watering companion to *The Daniel Plan* book and *The Daniel Plan Journal* to help transform your health in the most head-turning way imaginably—from the inside out.

## The Daniel Plan Journal

### 40 Days to a Healthier Life

*Rick Warren and The Daniel Plan Team*

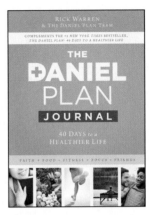

The Perfect Daniel Plan Companion for Better Overall Health

Research shows that tracking your food and exercise greatly contributes to your long-term success. Maximize your momentum by exploring and charting your journey through the five key Essentials of The Daniel Plan—Faith, Food, Fitness, Focus, and Friends.

Taking readers of *The Daniel Plan: 40 Days to a Healthier Life* to the next level, *The Daniel Plan Journal* is the perfect companion, providing encouraging reminders about your health. On the days you need a little boost, *The Daniel Plan Journal* has the daily Scripture, inspiration, and motivation you need to stay on track and keep moving forward.

*Available in stores and online!*

# The Daniel Plan Five Essentials Series

The Daniel Plan Five Essentials Series is an innovative approach to creating a healthy lifestyle, rooted and framed by five life areas: Faith, Food, Fitness, Focus, and Friends.

Host Dee Eastman and The Daniel Plan's founding doctors and wellness faculty—including Gary Thomas, Dr. Mark Hyman, Sean Foy, Basheerah Ahmad, Dr. Daniel Amen, and Dr. John Townsend—equip you to make healthy choices on a daily basis.

Each video session features not only great teaching but testimony from those who have incorporated The Daniel Plan into their everyday lives. A weekly Fitness Move and Food Tip are also provided. The study guide include icebreakers and review questions, video notes, video discussion questions, next steps suggestions, prayer starters, and helpful appendices.

The Daniel Plan has transformed thousands of people around the world and it can transform you as well.

*Available in stores and online!*

## The Daniel Plan in Action

40 Day Fitness Programs With
Dynamic Workouts

*Introduction by Rick Warren D. Min.*

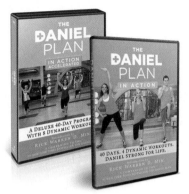

*The Daniel Plan in Action* is a 40-day fitness
system with an innovative approach to creating a
healthy lifestyle, rooted and framed by five life areas:
faith, food, fitness, focus and friends. Three expert instructors
lead the variety of inspiring workouts with a strong backbone of faith and
community, complemented by a soundtrack of exclusive Christian music. This
4-session and 8-session systems focus on an abundance of healthy choices
offering you the encouragement and inspiration you need to succeed.

*Go to DanielPlan.com now to learn more.*

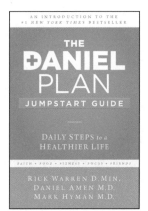

# The Daniel Plan Jumpstart Guide

Daily Steps to a Healthier Life

*Rick Warren D. Min., Daniel Amen M.D.,
Mark Hyman M.D.*

*The Daniel Plan Jumpstart Guide* provides a bird's-eye view of getting your life on track to better health in five key areas: Faith, Food, Fitness, Focus, and Friends. This booklet provides all the key principles for readers to gain a vision for health and get started—breaking out existing content from *The Daniel Plan: 40 Days to a Healthier Life* into a 40-day action plan. The *Jumpstart Guide* encourages readers to use *The Daniel Plan* and *The Daniel Plan Journal* for more information and further success.

*Available in stores and online!*